P9-CLJ-384

# CELTIC GLASS PAINTING

## JUDY BALCHIN

Gill & Macmillan

First published in Ireland 2000 by
Gill & Macmillan Ltd.
Hume Avenue, Park West, Dublin 12
with associated companies throughout the world
www.gillmacmillan.ie

ISBN 0 7171 3136 X

First published in Great Britain 2000 by
Search Press Limited
Wellwood, North Farm Road,
Tunbridge Wells, Kent TN2 3DR

Text copyright © Judy Balchin 2000

Photographs by Search Press Studios
Photographs and design copyright © Search Press Ltd. 2000

All rights reserved. No part of this book, text, photographs or
illustrations may be reproduced or transmitted in any form or by
any means by print, photoprint, microfilm, microfiche,
photocopier, internet or in any way known or as yet unknown, or
stored in a retrieval system, without written permission obtained
beforehand from Search Press.

The Publishers and author can accept no responsibility for any
consequences arising from the information, advice or instructions
given in this publication.

Readers are permitted to reproduce any of the items/patterns in
this book for their personal use, or for the purposes of selling for
charity, free of charge and without the prior permission of the
Publishers. Any use of the items/patterns for commercial
purposes is not permitted without the prior permission of the
Publishers.

**Suppliers**
If you have difficulty in obtaining any of the materials and
equipment mentioned in this book, then please visit the Search
Press website for details of suppliers: www.searchpress.com

Alternatively, you can write to the Publishers at the address
above, for a current list of stockists, which includes firms who
operate a mail-order service.

**Publishers' note**
All the step-by-step photographs in this book feature the
author, Judy Balchin, demonstrating how to paint on glass.
No models have been used.

Colour separation by Graphics '91 Pte Ltd, Singapore
Printed in Spain by Elkar S. Coop, 48180 Loiu (Bizkaia)

*I would like to thank John Wright of Pebeo UK Ltd., Unit 109,
Solent Business Centre, Millbrook, Southampton, SO15 OHW for
supplying the glass paints used in this book.*

*I would also like to thank Edding UK Ltd., Merlin Centre, Acrewood
Way, St Albans, Herts, AL4 0JY for supplying the Marabu Fun &
Fancy peel-off paint, and David Rabone of Regalead Ltd., Sharston
Road, Manchester, M22 4TH for providing the self-adhesive lead.*

*A big thank you goes to the team at Search Press. In particular to
Managing Director Martin de la Bédoyère for his vision; Editorial
Director Roz Dace and Editor Chantal Roser for their editorial
wisdom and guidance; Julie Wood for her sympathetic design skills
and Lotti de la Bédoyère for her photography.*

*Page 1*
**Knotwork cross**
*This Celtic cross is outlined with 3mm (0.120in) self-
adhesive lead and black outliner. It is then painted, and
embellished with gold outliner when dry.*

*Opposite*
**Bookmark**

*This design is outlined and painted on acetate, which can
also be used as a surface for glass paints. When dry, it is
glued on to card and cut out.*

# CONTENTS

# INTRODUCTION

The Celtic civilisation has exerted a more lasting influence than almost any other. It flourished in Europe before the Roman Empire and Christianity, lasting for over a thousand years from the sixth century BC to the ninth century AD. Today, Celtic languages are still spoken in Brittany, Ireland and parts of the British Isles, and the Celts' beautiful stylistic and intricate designs are as popular as ever.

Early Celts lived a pagan life, as farmers, warriors and artists, worshipping natural forms such as Mother Earth, the stars, the sun and the moon. Because of their oral tradition, they had no written records, but would memorise events, incorporating them into chants and prose. These were recited by bards, who entertained and educated the tribes. They in turn passed the mythology on from generation to generation. During this early period, artists worked in stone and metal, using their skills to create monuments, weapons and jewellery.

It was not until the fifth and sixth centuries AD that British and Irish monasteries were established and workshops set up to produce illuminated manuscripts and books. These now provide us with a wealth of Celtic artistry. A page might feature only one word, perhaps a capital letter, but this is infused with life – decorative motifs mixed with interlaced creatures, stylised figures, angels – and ornamentation purely from the artist's imagination.

My love of both Celtic design and glass painting has made writing this book a fascinating challenge. Celtic art is breathtaking and it is only after spending time working on the designs that I have begun to understand and appreciate the skill of the artists. Taking my inspiration from them, I have simplified and adapted their designs for glass painting, retaining, I hope, the energy and power of the original patterns and motifs. I have included spirals, knotwork and zoomorphic designs, as well as figures and initials – and painted them in glorious rich colours, gilding some and embellishing others. I hope you enjoy using this book and that you find the inspiration to go on and create your own Celtic designs.

*Opposite*
***Angel panel***
*You can include many glass painting and embellishment techniques on one piece of glass. This panel combines lead, outliner, painting, gilding, and embellishment with coloured stones and dots of gold outliner.*

# MATERIALS

Outliners, self-adhesive lead, glass paints and gilding products are available from all good art and craft outlets, and you should be able to find the rest of the materials in your own home. Because of the intricacy of Celtic design, you will have to choose your glass items carefully. The main thing to remember is to keep them simple. Clip frames are ideal as they are inexpensive and available in a variety of sizes. Alternatively, visit your local glazier who will be able to cut glass to size. Simple, chunky vases, goblets and bottles can be found in junk shops, DIY and kitchen outlets, supermarkets and gift shops.

## OUTLINERS

Designs need to be outlined first before they can be painted and there are various outliners available which are specifically designed for painting on glass. Raised lines are created when you pipe them on to the surface and these contain the paint within specific areas. Designs can also be outlined using a technical pen, although the lines produced will lie flat against the glass. Colours can be flooded over the drawn lines to seal the pen work. If you want a more authentic stained-glass appearance, self-adhesive lead is ideal. This is flexible and excellent when used for simple motifs and borders.

*There are various outliners available. I use a selection in this book and they are shown here:*

*1. Draughting film ink  This is used with a technical pen for drawing on a smooth surface.*

*2. Technical pen  You can outline or draw fine detail with this.*

*3. Black outliner  You can apply raised lines with this.*

*4. Metallic outliner  This is used to create raised outlines and decoration on painted pieces.*

*5. Boning tool  This is used to rub down self-adhesive lead.*

*6. Self-adhesive lead  Different widths are available. This can be used for simple designs and borders.*

*Black outliner accentuates the intricate pattern of this Celtic knot.*

## Black and imitation lead outliners

These outliners are supplied in tubes fitted with fine nozzles, so that raised lines can be applied to a glass surface easily. The paints will not colour these outlines. Blobs can form on the end of the nozzle when you are working, but these can easily be wiped away with absorbent paper. It is advisable to practise on paper or acetate before starting the projects. Lay the tip of the nozzle lightly on the surface and squeeze gently with an even pressure while pulling the tube along the surface; this will produce an even, unbroken line. It is easier to create straight lines by lifting the tube slightly off the surface. Cotton buds are useful for wiping away mistakes while the outliner is still wet. Alternatively errors can be scraped off with a knife when dry.

## Metallic outliners

Metallic outliners are applied in the same way as the black and imitation lead outliners. However, paint will colour the outlines, so you will have to take care when painting. Alternatively, you can outline your design in black, paint and complete the project, let it dry, then work over the black outline with the metallic outliner. Generally, I decorate my finished pieces with these outliners – this avoids the problem of the paint colouring them. They can also be sponged on to glass to add sparkle. Squeeze the outliner on to a palette and use a sponge to apply the paste with a dabbing motion.

*The Celtic knot is painted, then embellished with dots of gold outliner.*

*A technical pen is used to outline the design. The pen work is then sealed with solvent-based paints.*

## Technical pen

A technical pen can be used for outlining, even though it only produces a flat line. It is ideal for detailed work within an outlined panel. A 0.5mm (0.020in) nib is shown in this book, but the pens can be fitted with different sized nibs. You should use draughting film ink as this is designed to adhere to a smooth surface. Always make sure that your glass is really clean before outlining with a pen. Wipe the surface with methylated spirits to remove all traces of grease. As the ink used in the pen is water-based, it can easily be scratched off the surface of the glass. To overcome this problem, seal the pen work with either clear or coloured paint. Make sure that you use solvent-based paints, as water-based will remove the pen work. Apply them generously, flooding the area so that the pen work is completely sealed.

## Decorative self-adhesive lead

An authentic stained-glass look can be achieved using this lead. It is available from craft outlets and glaziers and is supplied on a roll in different widths. The 3mm (0.120in) width is supplied in a double ribbed strip which should be cut to create a fine outline; these fine strips can be used for simple designs and borders. The glass surface should be wiped clean with methylated spirits before you start and the lead should be cut on a cutting mat, using a scalpel. The paper backing is then peeled off to reveal the adhesive, and the lead is pressed on to the glass surface firmly.

The rolls are supplied with a plastic boning tool which is used to rub the lead firmly on to the glass.

A Celtic cross outlined with self-adhesive lead.

---

**HEALTH AND SAFETY WARNING**

*Personal hygiene is important when handling self-adhesive lead. Always wash your hands thoroughly before eating, drinking or smoking. The lead is safe to use if these simple precautions are observed.*

---

# GLASS PAINTS

Water-based and solvent-based glass paints are available from art and craft outlets. They are transparent and manufactured specifically for application to glass and other smooth surfaces. The majority of these paints are purely decorative and not intended for functional items, therefore care has to be taken when finished items are washed. Some water-based glass paints and outliners can be baked in a domestic oven, which makes them both durable and dishwasher safe. Always check the manufacturers' instructions carefully.

The paints are available in a wide variety of rich, vibrant colours and are intermixable within their range. However, solvent-based paints will not mix with water-based paints. Do not shake the bottles before you use them, as this will create air bubbles. Apply them liberally straight from the bottle to achieve a smooth stained-glass effect, then allow them to settle flat. Always make sure that your painted pieces are left to dry in a dust-free area, or cover them carefully with an upturned box.

## Water-based paints

These dry quickly and have little odour. Do not dilute them with water, as their viscosity will be affected. Dilute them instead with clear glass paint within the range you have selected. Some water-based paints can be baked in the oven to make them durable and dishwasher safe. Check the manufacturers' instructions and choose these if you are decorating anything that may come into contact with food and requires frequent washing. Brushes used with water-based paints can be cleaned in water.

## Solvent-based paints

These paints have a more antique appearance and are durable, although care still has to be taken when washing decorated items. They can be diluted with solvent-based clear glass paint; this can also be used to protect a finished piece, but you should wait at least a week before applying the protective coat. It is important to work in a well ventilated area when using these paints and brushes must be cleaned with white spirit.

You can also buy solvent-based ceramic paints, which are opaque. A truly flat finish can be created by painting or sponging the back of the glass with these paints (see page 26).

*Spiral design painted with solvent-based paints.*

*Celtic knot outlined and filled with peel-off paint.*

## Peel-off paint

These transparent water-based paints are supplied in bottles fitted with fine nozzles and they can be used to decorate glass, mirrors, ceramic ware and porcelain. They are available in a wide variety of colours and metallic effects, and include an outliner range. The paints are used in two stages. First the outlines are squeezed on to either a plastic pocket or a piece of glass and left to dry, then the colours are squeezed into the outlined areas directly from the bottles. Designs are then peeled away from the backing and can be applied to both two and three dimensional surfaces. The colours are opaque when they are first applied, but on drying they become transparent. They take approximately twenty four hours to dry.

9

## OTHER MATERIALS

You will not need all the items shown here when you start glass painting. The projects show exactly what you will need to complete each design.

1. **Cutting mat** Cut self-adhesive lead on a cutting mat.

2. **Masking tape** Used to secure patterns to glass before outlining.

3. **Ceramic paint** This is painted or sponged on to the back of glass to give a flat finish when viewed from the front.

4. **Oil paint** Burnt umber is used to age a gilded surface.

5. **Synthetic round paintbrushes** You will need Nos. 2 and 4 to apply the paint.

6. **Large soft brush** Used to brush away any loose leaf when gilding.

7. **Palette** Used for mixing colours.

8. **Pieces of sponge** Synthetic sponges are great for applying paint.

9. **White spirit** Clean brushes used with solvent-based paint with this.

10. **Methylated spirits** Used to clean glass.

11. **Strong clear glue** Attach glass droplets to glass with this.

12. **Water** Clean brushes used with water-based paint with this.

13. **Spray glue** Used to attach a paper pattern to a glass surface.

14. **Shellac** A coat will protect a gilded piece of work.

15. **Dutch metal leaf** Used for gilding. It is available in sheets with various metallic finishes.

16. **Gilding size** Used as an adhesive for Dutch metal leaf.

17. **Scissors** Cut out patterns with these.

18. **Scalpel** You should cut self-adhesive lead with this.

19. **White paper** Used as a backing when painting designs.

20. **Parchment paper** This can replace the backing sheet of a clip frame to give a more authentic look.

21. **Absorbent paper** Wipe nozzles and brushes, and mop up spills with this. It can also be used with methylated spirits to clean surfaces.

22. **Cotton buds** Wipe away outliner mistakes and correct small paint spills with these.

23. **Glass droplets** You can add decoration with these.

24. **Blanks** There are many blank items available that you can decorate – clip frames, goblets, plates and more.

25. **Plastic pockets** These are used as a base when working with peel-off paints.

26. **Technical pen** Outline or draw fine detail with this.

27. **Draughting film ink** Use this with the technical pen for drawing on a smooth surface.

28. **Boning tool** Used for smoothing and flattening self-adhesive lead on to glass.

# KNOTWORK

*Knotwork originates from three dimensional crafts
such as plaiting and weaving.
It was the Celtic craftsmen who took this
art to its extreme.*

# History

There are few cultures who have not used interlaced designs in their simplest form. Interwoven borders around a central image can be found in Greek, Roman and Egyptian art. This decoration originates from three dimensional crafts such as plaiting, weaving and basketry. However, it was the Celtic craftsmen who took the art to its extreme, creating the intricate knotwork that instantly evokes their culture. At first, the repetitive plaitwork design was used to cover areas of vellum and stone. Then interlaced knots were added to create more variety. These plaits and knots were first used to decorate the cross, a pattern frequently used by the Celts.

As Celtic craftsmen progressed with the complexity of their designs, pointed loops were introduced to fill corners of manuscripts and stonework, and knotwork was used to decorate more shapes, such as squares and triangles. The craftsmen and manuscript writers worked in isolated 'pockets' around Britain and Ireland. Because of this there were differences in their work, peculiar to their own locality. Some created an inline within the knot, others introduced interlaced rings to their work. Despite the differences, the symbolism in the knotwork remained the same. The unbroken lines of these interlaced decorations represented eternal spiritual growth.

Knotwork requires a steady hand and it can only be executed with great concentration. With its strong lines and vibrant colour, it lends itself perfectly to glass painting. Take your time when outlining the designs in this chapter. They look difficult, but in time you will find a rhythm in your work that makes the process quite therapeutic.

# Celtic corners

This project introduces you to peel-off paint, which is great fun to use. The designs are outlined then filled in with paint. When dry, they can be peeled off and applied to glass, metal and ceramics, on two and three dimensional surfaces. The paint is applied straight from the bottle and designs take approximately twenty-four hours to dry. The colours are milky at first, but they become transparent when dry. It is advisable not to peel them off before they are completely dry, or they may tear.

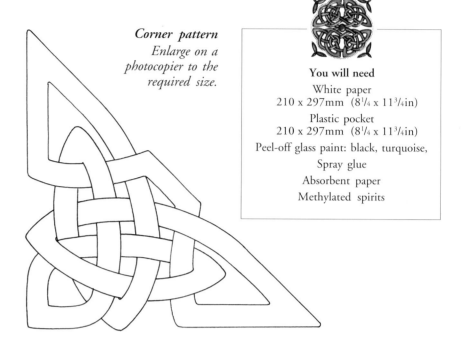

*Corner pattern*
*Enlarge on a photocopier to the required size.*

**You will need**
White paper
210 x 297mm (8$^1$/$_4$ x 11$^3$/$_4$in)
Plastic pocket
210 x 297mm (8$^1$/$_4$ x 11$^3$/$_4$in)
Peel-off glass paint: black, turquoise,
Spray glue
Absorbent paper
Methylated spirits

1. Photocopy the design four times. Cut each one out, then glue all four on to a sheet of white paper.

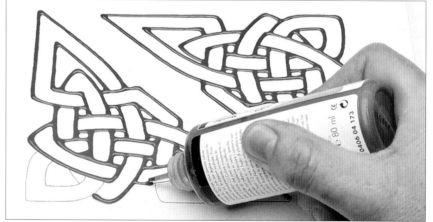

2. Slip the paper into a plastic pocket and smooth it flat to remove any trapped air. Using black, start at the top and outline each design. Keep wiping the tip of the nozzle with absorbent paper to prevent clogging. Also, make sure there are no gaps, or the design might tear when you remove it from the plastic pocket.

3. Use turquoise and carefully flood colour into the knotwork. Make sure that you fill in all the sections so there are no gaps. If air bubbles appear in the paint, prick them with a pin.

4. Fill in all the sections behind the knotwork with clear paint. This appears white when wet, but will become transparent as it dries.

5. Finish painting the four designs. Leave to dry for twenty-four hours, then carefully peel each one away from the plastic pocket.

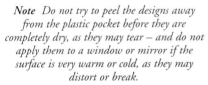

**Note** *Do not try to peel the designs away from the plastic pocket before they are completely dry, as they may tear – and do not apply them to a window or mirror if the surface is very warm or cold, as they may distort or break.*

*The designs may lose adhesion if they are moved several times. Just dampen the reverse sides with water and they will stick to the surface.*

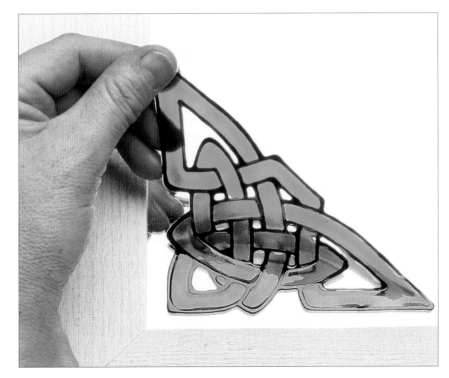

6. Clean the surface of a mirror or window with methylated spirits to remove any grease, then place one design in each corner. Press them on to the surface firmly.

*Opposite*
**Knotwork vase**
*Motifs using peel-off paint can be applied to three dimensional surfaces such as vases, bottles, jars and candlesticks. Use the techniques shown on the previous pages to create your own designs. Here, the central glass droplet is placed on the wet paint, and this acts as a glue when dry.*

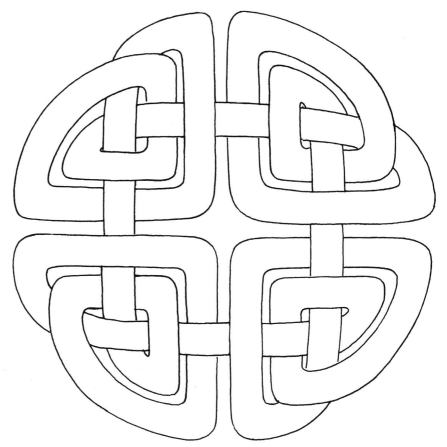

*Pattern for the knotwork vase opposite*

*Pattern for the Celtic chalice on page 18*

*Pattern for the gilded bowl on page 19*

17

*Above*
**Gilded bowl**

*Photocopy and enlarge the pattern several times. Join the pieces together with masking tape to form a strip that will fit inside your bowl, then outline and paint the design. Gild the inside and seal it with clear varnish (see pages 48 and 49).*

*Opposite*
**Celtic chalice**

*With a little outliner and paint you can transform a plain glass goblet into a beautiful Celtic chalice. Enlarge and photocopy the pattern enough times to form a continuous strip that will fit around the rim.*

*Patterns for the knotwork designs opposite*

*Knotwork designs*

# ZOOMORPHICS

*It is obvious that the Celtic scribes enjoyed creating these fantastic zoomorphic designs, as they seem to spring from their pages with raw energy.*

# HISTORY

Zoomorphics are designs based on the forms of animals, birds and reptiles. These beings were sacred to the Celts and many of them were used to represent their gods and spirits. Christ was identified by a large number of symbolic animals such as the fish, snake, lion and peacock.

Interlocking zoomorphic designs were popular with Celtic sculptors, and there are also some beautiful painted examples in the Book of Kells. This gospel book was written in the eighth century, two hundred years after the death of St. Columba, who founded the monasteries in Ireland. It is believed that the book was written as a celebration of his life and devotion to the scriptures. Perhaps it was his great love of animals that inspired the prolific use of zoomorphic decoration.

If necessary, Celtic artists could produce recognisable zoomorphics, but when the opportunity arose, they loved nothing better than to distort and elaborate on the basic form. In manuscript pages dogs chase each other, biting the tails of those in front; birds interweave their necks and bodies and are even illustrated with cats' heads; snakes intertwine and turn into elaborate interlaced, knotworked patterns. It is obvious that the scribes enjoyed these fantastic creations, as they seem to spring from the pages with raw energy.

So let us recreate the vitality and energy of these fascinating forms with the following project – a circular gold design set against a rich, dark blue background on a decorative Celtic plate.

# DECORATIVE PLATE

A technical pen is used in this project. With its fine nib you can achieve beautifully detailed work, which would be difficult with an outliner. The design is drawn on to the back of a glass plate, then opaque ceramic paints are used to block in the design. The surface is then sponged, thus sealing in the fine pen work. When the plate is viewed from the front, it has a truly professional appearance. This design has a vitality which is enhanced by the choice of gold against a dark background. The dogs chase each other around a central motif in a never-ending dance, full of life and energy.

**You will need**

Glass plate
White paper
Technical pen, fitted with a 0.5mm (0.020in) nib
Draughting film ink
Self-adhesive lead 3mm (0.120in) wide
Boning tool
Solvent-based ceramic paints: gold, dark blue
No. 2 paintbrush
Newspaper
Pieces of sponge
Palette
Cutting mat and scalpel
Spray glue
Absorbent paper
Methylated spirits

**Pattern for the decorative plate**
*Increase or decrease the size on a photocopier so that it will fit comfortably within the flat base of your plate. All the work is done on the back of the plate, so this design will be reversed when viewed from the front.*

1. Lightly spray the front of the pattern with glue, then press it face down on to the centre of the plate.

*Note* *Always clean a glass surface with methylated spirits before working with a technical pen, so that the ink adheres to the surface. It is easy to remove mistakes using a damp cotton bud.*

2. Turn the plate over and wipe the surface with methylated spirits. Outline the border with a technical pen. Leave to dry. Outline the central motif. Leave to dry.

3. Replace the pattern with a circle of white paper. Using a No. 2 paintbrush and gold paint, work on the back of the plate and paint the central motif. Apply the colour generously and carefully work round the border, filling it all in. Leave to dry for twenty four hours.

4. Remove the white paper. Lay a sheet of newspaper over the work surface to protect it. Place the plate on a roll of tape to lift it up slightly, then pour dark blue paint into a palette and sponge it on to the back of the plate. This will create air bubbles but these will disperse. Leave to dry for twenty four hours, then sponge on another coat of dark blue.

5. Turn the plate over and measure a strip of lead slightly larger than the circumference. Cut it, pull off the backing and stick it around the edge, leaving a slight overlap at the join.

6. Rub the lead flat with the boning tool, working round the edge of the plate with smooth movements until you meet the overlap.

7. Cut through both of the thicknesses in the centre of the overlapping section.

8. Remove the end of the overlapping top section and discard it.

9. Carefully peel back the rest of the top overlap. Remove the bottom section.

10. Butt the two ends together and rub the ends smooth with the boning tool.

*Decorative plate*

*This plate is backpainted, which creates a beautifully flat finish when viewed from the front. The energy of the zoomorphic design is captured in the brilliance of the gold, as the dogs ceaselessly chase each other against the opaque blue background.*

Pattern for the red and gold plate opposite.
All the work is done on the back of the plate, so the design will
be reversed when viewed from the front.

**Red and gold plate**
The inspiration for this design is taken from the symbol for St Luke – the calf
as represented in the Book of Kells. It is possible to achieve the fine detailing on
the wings and body if you use a technical pen.

*Patterns for the zoomorphic designs opposite*

*Zoomorphic designs*

# SPIRALS

*The central spiral rotates in the opposite direction to the outer spirals, helping to create a sense of calm and stillness at the core of these swirling patterns.*

# HISTORY

Shells were used as vessels by our earliest ancestors and nature's spirals inspired people long before the Celts started to develop them into beautiful swirling designs. The people of Asia, Africa, Europe, Polynesia and the Americas all used the one-coil spiral as decoration. This has been found on monuments, carved into stone balls and sculpted into rocks in isolated areas. The siting of the designs suggests that they marked ritual centres or burial grounds. Some of them were aligned with the winter solstice, which also suggests that they may have been solar symbols.

The elaborate Celtic spirals radiate out from the centre, creating a triskele or swastika in the middle. The heart of the spiral is sometimes filled with knotwork patterns and spirals could be linked together to create borders or to produce lozenge and triangular shapes. Spiral work was particularly popular in the decoration of jewellery and weaponry. Fantastic sword hilts and bracelets were embossed with intricate swirling patterns.

The key to Celtic spiral work was balance. The Celts lived surrounded by water and were constantly reminded of the flow of life and the planets as they toiled to reach this balance. If you study the designs, you will see that the central spiral rotates in the opposite direction to the outer spirals, helping to create a sense of calm at the core of the swirling patterns.

In this chapter, you are invited to bring a sense of calm and balance into your home by decorating one of your windows with a colourful panel. The swirling spirals lend themselves perfectly to glass painting. You can also decorate three dimensional objects, such as vases or bottles.

# WINDOW PANEL

I am frequently asked how to paint a design on a vertical window. Glass paint runs, so it is far easier to work on a flat glass panel, then you can fix your design to the window with self-adhesive lead – an easy answer to a difficult problem. Also, if you move house, simply remove the lead and take the panel with you!

In the pattern opposite, the thicker lines show you where to place the self-adhesive lead. Glass can be cut to size at a glaziers. Make sure that the panel fits comfortably within your existing window.

**You Will Need**
Circular 2mm (0.080in) glass panel with smoothed edges, 34cm (13½in) diameter
Masking tape
Self-adhesive lead: 3mm(0.120in) wide double-ribbed and 9mm (³/₈in) wide flat
Boning tool
Outliner: black
Technical pen, fitted with a 0.5mm(0.020in) nib
Draughting film ink
White paper
Solvent-based paints: yellow, orange, blue, green, red, clear
No. 4 paintbrush
Cutting mat
Scalpel
Absorbent paper
Methylated spirits
Strong clear glue
3 small blue glass droplets
1 large blue glass droplet

1. Place the glass panel on top of the pattern. Use small pieces of masking tape to secure the edges. Clean the surface with methylated spirits.

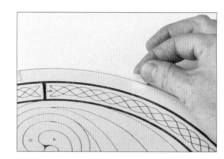

2. Cut a 7cm (2³/₄in) length of 3mm (0.120in) lead. Cut down the centre rib and remove the backing paper from one length. Press the strip on to the glass over one of the three outer spokes. Cut to fit. Repeat twice more on the remaining spokes.

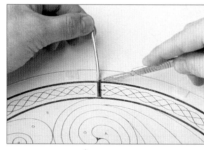

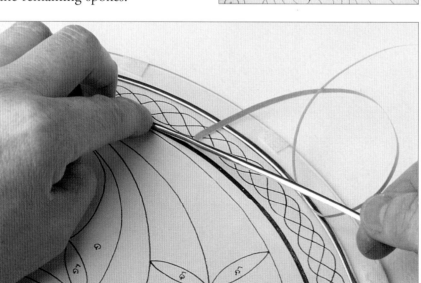

3. Cut a 100cm (39¼in) length of 3mm (0.120in) lead. Cut it down the centre with a scalpel and remove the paper backing from one strip. Place it round the outer circle. Trim the other strip to 90cm (35½in) and remove the backing. Press it round the inner circle.

***Pattern for the window panel***

*Enlarge on a photocopier to fit your window.*

1 ~ Yellow

2 ~ Orange

3 ~ Amber – *mix equal quantities of orange and yellow*

4 ~ Blue

5 ~ Green

6 ~ Light green – *mix clear paint with a little green*

7 ~ Red

4. Rub the lead borders and spokes firmly down on to the glass with the boning tool. Trim the ends.

5. Run the tip of the boning tool round all the edges to seal the lead to the glass.

6. Use black outliner to outline the central spiral, then the three outer spirals and leaves. If blobs form on the end of the nozzle, wipe them away with absorbent paper and continue working. Leave to dry for thirty minutes.

7. Clean the outer border area with methylated spirits. Trace the pattern with a technical pen. Leave to dry for a few minutes.

8. Remove the pattern and place the panel on white paper. Using the colour guide (see page 35), paint the central spiral using a No. 4 paintbrush and yellow, orange and amber. Use the same colours to paint the three outer spirals. Apply the paints liberally straight from the bottle, allowing the colours to settle flat within the outlines. Leave to dry.

9. Paint all the green areas, then paint all the blue areas.

10. Mix green with clear paint and fill in all the light green areas.

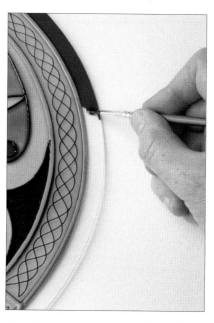

11. Seal the interlaced border with light green. Apply the paint generously to seal the pen work.

12. Paint the three small circles and the outer border red. Leave to dry.

13. Glue a large glass droplet on to the central circle. Glue three smaller droplets into place using the dotted circles on the pattern as a guide. Leave to set.

14. Cut a 110cm (43¼in) length of 9mm (³⁄₈in) lead with the scalpel. Press this round the edge of the panel so that 2mm (0.080in) is sticking to the glass with 7mm (¼in) hanging over the edge. Use the boning tool to rub the 2mm (0.080in) edge firmly on to the glass.

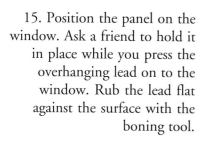

15. Position the panel on the window. Ask a friend to hold it in place while you press the overhanging lead on to the window. Rub the lead flat against the surface with the boning tool.

**Window panel**
*As the sun shines through this vibrant spiral panel, your room will be bathed in colour.*

### Gilded bottle

A plain glass bottle is transformed into a Celtic treasure with some outliner and a few sheets of Dutch metal leaf. It is then aged with oil paint and embellished with gems.

*Pattern for the gilded bottle*

*Opposite*

### Celtic vase

Self-adhesive lead is used to extend the decoration on this large vase. Keep the leaded lines simple to contrast with the complex painted spiral.

*Pattern for the Celtic vase opposite*

*Patterns for the spiral designs opposite*

*Spiral designs*

# FIGURES

*Copying the work of the Creator exactly was forbidden. This is the reason for the stylised representations of the human figure in Celtic art.*

# HISTORY

The figurative designs found in Celtic art were influenced by pagan law. This forbad the exact copying of the work of the Creator, which is the reason for the stylised representations of the human figure in Celtic art. We can only wonder at the stiff, solemn characters that stare out at us from the pages. Indeed, the monks' lives were hard, but they were not serious all the time, and they were definitely not averse to humour. If you look at the characters with their elongated limbs, tugging each other's beards and intertwining themselves with animals and birds, you wonder whether this was a method used by the monks to avoid exact representation. Or was it simply their sense of fun and mischief showing through?

In the majority of cases, figures were used purely as ornamental motifs. Where they represented a real person, the portrait was only commenced if the subject had passed away. It was a heinous crime to paint a portrait of a living person.

There are very few depictions of women in Celtic art, which comes as no surprise when you consider the male-dominated society in which the monks lived. I have only found two examples: a Samaritan woman holding a cup of water for Christ, and a wonderful depiction of the Virgin Mary and Child which can be found in the Book of Kells. I have taken the latter as my inspiration for the following project, in which the images of Mother and Child are outlined, gilded and antiqued.

# VIRGIN MARY AND CHILD

The decorative work on this embossed panel gives a wonderful rich texture to the surface – and all you need is outliner to create the raised design. This is covered with sheets of Dutch metal leaf and aged with oil paint. The panel can then be painted with glass paints (see page 51), or left as a gilded design. If you are new to outlining, try completing one section, then let it dry before moving on to the next. If you do this, you will avoid smudging the wet paste with your hand. Also, make sure that your outline is well raised so that you create a good, effective base for the gilding.

Before you start, dismantle the frame. Photocopy the pattern opposite, slip it under the glass, then reassemble the frame.

**You will need**
Clip frame
210 x 297mm (8¼ x 11¾in)
Outliner: gold
Gilding size
4 sheets of Dutch metal gold leaf
Large soft brush
Shellac
Oil paint: burnt umber
Strong clear glue
2 coloured glass droplets

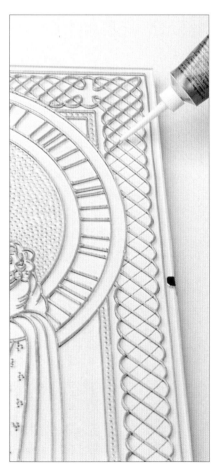

1. Carefully outline the figures with gold outliner, starting at the top and working down. Outline the halo and the inner circle, then fill this area with small dots of outliner.

2. Outline the rest of the design, except for the Celtic knot border. Leave to dry. Outline all the border diagonals in one direction. Leave to dry, then outline the remaining diagonals.

*Pattern for the Virgin Mary and Child*
*Enlarge on a photocopier by 120%*

3. Check that all your outlines are well raised so that the relief work is effective. If some areas are not raised enough, carefully add more outliner. Leave to dry.

4. Remove the clips from the frame. Paint the whole surface with gilding size. Allow it to dry until it becomes clear.

5. Carefully lay four sheets of gold leaf over the panel, overlapping them slightly. Press them gently down on to the design with your fingers to flatten them over the outlines, so that they adhere to the size. Leave to dry for thirty minutes.

6. Brush off loose pieces of leaf with a large soft brush. Fill in any gaps or cracks with size and small pieces of gold leaf.

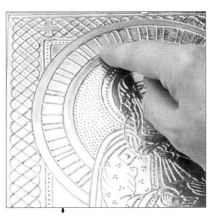

7. Apply one coat of Shellac to protect the gilding. Leave to dry for twenty-four hours.

8. Rub the surface with burnt umber oil paint using your finger. This will antique the gilding. Leave to dry.

9. Glue two glass droplets in the centre of the crosses in the bottom two squares.

**Virgin Mary and Child**

*This is certainly a test for your outlining skills, but it is definitely well worth the effort! The embossed panel glows and changes as light passes across the gilded surface.*

**Virgin Mary and Child**

*Take the panel one step further by painting the design with diluted solvent-based paints. The gilding shines through the transparent colours.*

51

*Pattern for the design opposite.*

52

**The four horsemen**
*You can bring together figurative and knotwork designs to create an elaborate panel. Self-adhesive lead, outliners, glass paints and coloured gems are all used to transform a plain piece of glass.*

*Patterns for the figurative designs opposite.*

*Figurative designs*

55

# INITIALS

*As the art of the manuscript developed, letters*
*were ornamented with interlacing knotwork*
*designs. Later initials bore unfurling spirals.*

## HISTORY

The script used in Celtic manuscripts was derived from classic, rounded Roman half uncials. Writing on vellum with goose feathers, scribes working on The Book of Kells actually completed sections quite quickly, finishing six lines in approximately fifteen minutes. The work was laborious and strenuous, and the silent monks occasionally scribbled notes in the margins – perhaps messages to neighbouring scribes. One monk wrote 'I am cold and weary, ink is bad, vellum is rough and wrinkled, the day is dark'. These words give us a real insight into the lives they led. It must have been a welcome relief to work on the beautifully illuminated letters at the beginning of the written sections.

Early manuscript initials were painstakingly embellished with tiny red dots which followed the contours of the forms. Letters were decorated purely with colour. As the art of the manuscript developed, they were ornamented with interlacing knotwork designs and panels. Later initials bore unfurling spirals, zoomorphic and figurative designs. Writhing animals and birds twined themselves in and around the letters, heads emerging at the terminals, with their tongues creating even more interlaced decoration.

The ornate capital R, which forms the next project, combines both knotwork and zoomorphic ornamentation. Inspired by the manuscripts produced by the monks so long ago, I have created a truly elaborate illuminated panel.

# ILLUMINATED INITIAL

I can already hear the gasps of delight, then horror, as you turn to this page. Celtic initials are incredibly striking, but the beauty of them lies in their intricacy. Do not be put off by the complexity of the design. If you divide the project into four main stages – outlining, pen work, painting and embellishment, it is not too daunting. This is a panel created to be hung on a wall. The light will not shine through the glass, so some of the denser colours have been diluted with clear glass paint to lighten them. If you insert parchment paper behind the painted initial, the panel will look more authentic.

Before you start, dismantle the frame. Photocopy the pattern, slip it under the glass, then reassemble the frame. Wipe the surface with methylated spirits to remove any grease before outlining, and before drawing in the fine lines with the technical pen.

### You will need
Clip frame
210 x 297mm (8¼ x 11¾in)
Outliners: black, gold
Technical pen, fitted with a 0.5mm
(0.020in) nib
Draughting film ink
Solvent-based paints: yellow, red,
orange, turquoise, pink, green,
clear
Parchment paper
210 x 297mm (8¼ x 11¾in)
Self-adhesive lead, brass effect:
3mm (0.120in)
Boning tool
Cutting mat and scalpel
No. 2 paintbrush
Methylated spirits
Absorbent paper

*Pattern for the initial*
*Enlarge on a photocopier by 200%*

1. Outline the thick lines with black outliner. Leave to dry.

2. Draw in the fine lines with a technical pen. Leave to dry.

3. Replace the pattern with white paper. Dilute yellow paint with approximately 50% of clear paint. Flood the inner panels to seal the pen work.

4. Use a No. 2 paintbrush to paint the inner border red. Dilute turquoise with a small quantity of clear paint. Fill in the outer border and the area behind the bird.

5. Paint the dogs' tongues and the knotwork at the base of the initial yellow.

6. Use green mixed with a small quantity of clear paint, then orange, to paint the dog's heads at the top and base of the letter. Do not paint the eyes. Finally, use orange to paint the curl at the end of the initial's tail.

7. Use pink, yellow and diluted green to paint the bird within the loop. Leave to dry for twenty-four hours.

8. Pipe rows of small gold dots around the pen work design, over the turquoise border and round the edge of the initial.

9. Cut a 30cm (11³⁄₄in) and a 22cm (8³⁄₄in) length of 3mm (0.120in) self-adhesive lead. Cut along the middle groove of both pieces to make four thin strips. Press each one round the edge of the frame, then rub them down firmly on to the surface with the boning tool.

10. Carefully trim each corner with a scalpel. Slip a sheet of parchment paper behind the painted design before reassembling the clip frame.

**Illuminated initial**
*Use a Celtic initial to personalise a design for a special occasion.*

*Patterns for the illuminated initial designs opposite*

*Illuminated initial designs*

# Index